# THE
# CHRONICLES OF THE
# AFRICAN AMERICAN

HERBERT STRIDER

Published in the United States of America

Brilliant Books Literary
137 Forest Park Lane Thomasville
North Carolina 27360 USA

ISBN:
Paperback: 979-8-88945-280-5
Ebook: 979-8-88945-281-2

# ACKNOWLEDGEMENT

I would like to give thanks to God for the ability, strength, and knowledge he has given me to accomplish this task. My wife who encouraged me to write, and the Wendy Williams Show, which gave me a course for this journey.

I did my research online using internet explorer in the area of African American History Timeline, African American History in the Old West Timeline, which led me to a treasure trove of knowledge the Black Past.Org for the source of information, and cross-referencing with Wicki apedia

# INTRODUCTION

I would like to take you on a journey, a chronological journey through time of the African Americans in this country. This journey procede year by year, sometimes month by month, and day by day as we follow the life of the African American. This journey is about where we came from in Africa, and why we were brought to this country. Also, how the African came to the New World, and the contributions made by the African Americans to help build this nation. We will look at the laws that affected the African Americans, in and out of slavery. The journey will illustrate some of the positive, and some negative events in history, as well as, some of the movers and the shakers in the African American's quest for equality. This is also a brief history of our nation from the north, south, east, and west of our beloved nation. On this journey we will see accomplishments and set backs, however, most of all, you will see a people with a strong faith in God, and a passionate will to be free and equal. We will also encounter people with a vision, a vision to see around the next bend, over the next hill, and sometimes across the next river. The African Americans are a proud race of people, who have made very significant contributions to make our nation strong, even through harsh trial and tribulations. This journey will reveal where as a nation they started, how as a people, they developed, and where they are headed to make a better United States of America.

# CHAPTER 1

# OUR JOURNEY

O ur journey begins on the coast of West Africa, a very long time ago. The West Africans were mariners, merchants, fishermen, and farmers. These Africans have sailed great distances, and there is evidence of their travels as far as present day Mexico. Where the Indians, during the Olmec era, have made stone carvings of people of African ancestry, as far back as 800BCE. The African merchants had sailed into the ports of Holland, Spain Portugal, England, and France to trade with the Europeans in Gold, Ivory, and slaves, even though, gold and ivory were more profitable than slaves. On the western coast of Africa, there was two massive empires the Dahomey (currently Benin) and the Ashanti (currently Ghana). The inhabitants of these empires were fisherman, mariners, and merchants, which had sea ports at Qurdah and Elmina. The two empires flourished, and acquired much wealth in the trade of their fellow Africans. The African rulers and merchants were the middle men and thr real slave traders. The passive, unaware Africans were subjected to bondage by the brutal, gun-toting European sla-vers. The Atlantic coast of Africa was dangerous for the Europeans, because of the seasonal winds, which generated heavy surf, and treacherous crosscurrents, which pounded the shores that lacked any natural harbors, and hazardous offshore reefs and sandbars, which made navigating horrible. So, the Europeans would anchor far from the shore. They depended upon the skilled African sailors, known as canoe-men, to navigate the treacherous waters between the ships and the shore. The Europeans quest to obtain slaves was impeded by malaria, dysentery, yellow fever, and other diseases. They called the West Coast of Africa "white man's grave". In the early slave trade, the European merchants rarely called the shots. The Europeans needed the West African rulers, and merchants to gain access to the commodities they desired, especially slaves, and when they first started trading relationships with the West Africans in the mid 15th Century, the Europeans were amazed at the well-established and highly developed organizations and competitive commercial networks that had existed in Africa. Although, most West African societies didn't recognize private property in land, and the slave worked only as profitable means of production. The West Africans acquired wealth was in terms of dependent people, such as relatives, clients, or slaves. The Caravan routes linked the sub-Saharan Africans with North Africa, the Mediterranean, and the Middle East. Slavery in West Africa was well established prior to the European arrival. The West African rulers and merchants capitalized on the supply and demand of slaves, which was a byproduct of local warfare, kidnapping, or the manipulation of religious and judicial institutions. By the way, slavery was different to the African slaveholder, than to the European, for example, the African slave were in indentured servitude, the slave retained some rights, and their children were born free. The slave could be released from servitude by joining the clan as a warrior, or marry into the clan, but the Europeans claimed all slaves a property, and stripped them of all rights, and the children of slaves would also be a slave. Renown author Zayde Antrim quoted "African complicity in the slave trade neither justifies today's social problems nor minimizes their seriousness".

Through the years, the plague had devastated Europe, and the Europeans started to rebuild after plague with eyes on the New World. The King of Spain seeking riches, from across the waters in the New World, financed Christopher Columbus voyage to the New World. Columbus acquired a ships and crews, and among his crew were some free Africans, and his trusty Navigator, Pedro Alonso Nino, an African Moor, who had sailed the waters of the Atlantic. So, Columbus sailed from Spain in 1492. He supplied the ship in Porto Rico, Cuba, and finally arriving on an island that he named Hispaniola, (present day Haiti) in 1494. When he returned to Spain, Columbus had gold , spices, sugar cane, and Indian natives. The King ordered Columbus to return to Hispaniola with slaves to establish colonies. He arrived in Hispaniola with a ship full of slave in 1511. But nine year later, the slaves revolted, because of ill treatment, and staged the first slave uprising in the New World.

The King of Spain sent many explorers to establish colonies in the New World, such as Vasco Nunez de Balboa, who sailed throughout the Pacific Ocean in 1513, and among his crew was 30 Africans. Moreover, between the years 1522 and 1526, many Spanish explorers travel into the North America, such as, Juan Ponce de Leon, who was the first European to come the Southern part of the United states, with free and enslaved people 1511. Also, Pedro Menendez de Aviles, who founded St. Augustine, in Florida in 1565, which is the oldest established settlement in the United States, but at St. Augustine's settlement the Africans deserted the settlement to live with the Indians, and these Africans are considered the first to have settled in the United States. The Spanish explored from the Southwestern United States, as far as, the lower Mississippi River Valley, into Kansas, and New Mexico, where many Africans remained. During this period, the Spanish Crown abolishes slavery of the Native Americans, but not the Africans, although, the Africans were among the founders and early settlers of numerous towns, such as, in Texas, New Mexico, and California. The various towns, include, Laredo, El Paso, and San Antonio in Texas; Albuquerque in New Mexico, Tucson, Arizona, and in California, San Diego, Monterey, and San Francisco.

With the Spanish explorers in the South and Southwest, the Dutch and the French came from the North. Yet, four years before the settlement in Jamestown, Virginia, Mathieu Da Costa, a free black explorer, hired by the Dutch to guide the French explorers through parts of Canada and Lake Champlain, what is now upper New York state.

And when the English came to Jamestown and settled, they purchased 20 black indentured servants to assist the English in the Jamestown settlement. These Africans were the first in the English North American colonies in 1619. In 1620, the Pilgrims reached the New World, with Africans. Four years after their arrival, the first African birth is recorded in the English colonies. The child was born free, and was named William Tucker, who was baptized in Virginia.

When the Dutch West India Company, began to arrive in New York, they settled in and established the settlement of New Amsterdam (currently New York City), the Dutch, through the Dutch Slave Trade, had 11 African slaves, and the slaves quickly became the city's first municipal work force, clearing the land of timber, cutting lumber, cultivating crops, building roads and fortifications.

Samuel Maverick, a slaveholder from England, arrived with in Boston, Massachusetts in 1624, with two of his slaves, Tituba, who went to Salem, and Phillis Wheatley, who stayed in Boston, and is the first slaveholder in Massachusetts Colony. Massachusetts Colony had become important in the early days of slavery in the colonies, because it was the first colony to enact a slave law, also the first slaves imported into this country

Directly from Africa was through Massachusetts in 1634. Three and a half years later, the slave ship named Desire, brought the first shipment of slaves to the colonies from Barbados in exchange for Pequot Indians from New England. Also, Massachusetts Colony was the first to legalize slavery, when in 1641, Governor John Winthrop, a slave owner, with the Massachusetts Body of Liberties, also slave owners, drafted the law enslaving Africans. Many colonies adopted laws legalizing slavery, so in 1644, the Triangle Trade began, when Boston merchants started importing slaves directly from Africa, via the West Indies, to obtain sugar cane to produce rum. During which time in 1645, the Dutch colonist transferred some of their landholdings in New Amsterdam to their former slaves in compensation for their support in battling the Indians, but they were required to give a specific amount of produce from the land to their former owners. However, in Virginia 1651, an African American freeman named Anthony Johnson purchased several slaves and imported them to the Virginia Colony with him. The Virginia Colony gave him a land grant on Virginia's Puwgoteague River, so in turn, other free African Americans followed the same pattern. Moreover, Anthony Johnson eventually sued the Virginia Colony, because the court freed his slave John Casor, thinking that he was indentured. Anthony Johnson won his case and his slave was returned to him in 1655. Well, in 1652, the Massachusetts Colony passed a statute prohibiting blacks from being armed or trained for the militia, but had to resend it in 1656. After this action, the states of New York, and New Hampshire soon followed.

The slave laws became more strict as each colony enacted their state laws, so by 1663, the Maryland Colony enacted a slave law requiring all Africans arriving in the colony, whether, free or slave, will be put into bondage, and the European women married are married to an enslaved man, also will be put into bondage, and their children will, also, be enslaved. Many colonies adopted similar laws. And in South Carolina that year, the colony was giving every new settler coming into the colony a grant of 20 acres of land for each African male slave, and 10 acres of land for each African female slave, they bring into the colony. That year, also, the Virginia Colony clearly defines "enslavement is for life, and is transferred to the children through the mother. Black and slave becomes synonymous, and enslaved Africans are subject to harsher and more brutal control than other labors". And thus, the brutal subjugation of the African American begins. Some of the colonies enacted slave laws banning interracial marriages, restricting the travel of blacks, banning weapons or signaling devices, such as, horns or whistles, and Christians were also enslaved, and enslaved children were sold separately, African Americans could engage in any trade or commerce. In a six year period, between 1664 and 1700, slavery became more brutal and harsher for African Americans with no limits.

The 1700s had a few gains and many setbacks the the African slave. However, in 1711, the Pennsylvania Colony tried to end slavery, but Queen Anne of England refused. Also that year in New York

City, a public slave market is opened at the east end of Wall Street, and the next year, a slave revolt broke out, and many African slaves were killed. And by 1713, England acquired exclusive rights from Spain to transport African slaves to the Spanish colonies in America. After that, the French imported slaves in 1716, and two years later, New Orleans was founded, although, by 1721, there would be more black slaves in New Orleans than free white men. The period between 1721 thru 1737, saw the colonies strip the Africans of more rights, and the brutality, degradation, and disrespect for human rights increased throughout the colonies, so much as, in South Carolina the most extensive slave law was enforced, when the South Carolina Colony banned the teaching of slaves to read and write, also prohibited group assembly, and a black couldn't earn money for their work, it also permits a slaveholder to kill rebellious slaves.

# CHAPTER 2

# HOW WE HELPED
# BUILD A NATION

With the expansion of our nation moving westward, the Ohio State Constitution of 1802 outlawing slavery, but aggressively barred blacks from entering the state. Also, in 1802, in Virginia, James Callender, a journalist, claimed that Thomas Jefferson had several children by a slave concubine Sally Hemings. His claim was published in the Federalist newspaper and circulated around the country.

April 30, 1803, Louisiana was purchased by the French , and the new territory nearly doubles the size of the United States. However, In Vermont that year, Lemuel Haynes was the first African American to receive an honorary degree in U. S. history, when Middlebury College awards him a Master's Degree at its second commencement.

The Lewis and Clark Expedition of the newly acquired Louisiana and the Pacific Northwest territories began in 1804. And interestingly, an African American named York accompanied the expedition. He was the slave and childhood companion of William Clark, also an invaluable contribution to the expedition. He had risked his life to save Clark in a flash flood on the Missouri River near the Great Falls in present-day Montana. York hunted, helped with the set up and tear down of the camp. He assisted with all the tasks the other men performed. The Indians were curious, because they had never seen a black man before, although they had seen many white trappers. York was accepted very well among by Native Americans.

More African Americans were moving west, particulary Edward Rose, one of the many black fur trappers, who had traveled up the Missouri River to the Rocky Mountains in 1806, and he was one of many black trappers and fur trappers that explored the Rocky Mountains.

Meanwhile, on the East Coast, New Jersey deprived the African American of the voter's rights in 1807. Yet, in 1808, the United States government abolished the importation of African slaves, by enacting the "Slave Importation Ban". However, the Ban was widely ignored, because approximately 250, 000 blacks were still illegally imported. Also, that year, New York recognizes marriages within the African American community.

The United States census in 1810 revealed a national population of 7, 239, 881 residents with a black population of 1, 377, 808, including 186, 446 free African Americans.

The U. S. Congress, in 1810, banned African Americans from carrying mail for the U. S. Postal Service. Also, the state of Delaware had a black population of about 75 percent in, having the largest percentage of free blacks in a slave state. Moreover, in Philadelphia, the first African American Insurance Company, owned and operated by blacks opened their doors.

Massachusetts, in 1811, incorporated the previously independent black schools, into the Boston public school system.

When, The War of 1812 broke out, two black regiments was formed in New York to fight in the war. Over 600 black troops were part of the 3, 000 troops under General Andrew Jackson, who defeated the British forces at the Battle of New Orleans. The black troops were led by Major Joesph Savary, the highest black officer in the history of the U. S. Army by 1814.

The African Methodist Episcopal Church, the first black church denomination in the United States, is officially opened in 1815.

Also that year, Levi Coffin, an abolitionist from Indiana, began the Underground Railroad. The Underground Railroad spread across the North with routes originating in the South, which stretched to British Canada providing escape routes for slaves seeking freedom.

Francis Johnson, of Philadelphia, is the first African American bandleader to compose, and publish sheet music in 1817, and in 1837, becomes the first American to perform before Queen Victoria in England. During the years 1817 thru 1818, escaped slaves from Georgia, South Carolina, and Alabama joined the military campaign of the Florida Seminole Indians to keep their homelands. Also in 1818, Connecticut put a ban on black voters.

The United States census in 1820, revealed a population of 9, 638, 452 residents with a black population of 1, 771, 656, including 233, 504 free African Americans.

The Missouri Compromise of 1820 allowed Missouri into the Union as a slave state, and Maine as a free state. The boundary between a slave and free territory in the West was set at the 361h parallel. Free African Americans from the United States were able to settle in Mexican Texas in 1820, and in Texas 1822, the first cotton plantation with slaves in the United States was established, called Bernardo, founded by a former Georgia resident named Jared E. Groce, and it was on the Brazos River.

However, many African Americans were prospering during this period, especially, Thomas Jennings of New York City who was the first African American to receive a patent from the United Stated in 1821. He invented the first dry cleaning process of clothes. In New York, also, the African Grove Theater Group is founded. It is the first black acting company in the United States.

James Beckwourth, the most famous of the black fur trappers and trapper, when in 1825 began an exploration of the Rocky Mountains for the first time. He was also a member of William Henry Ashley's Fur Trading Expedition.

The first African American newspaper was published in New York City in 1827, with John Russwurm and Samuel Cornish are editors.

Also that year, slavery is abolished in New York state.

Theodore Sedgewick was the first African American to graduate from Princeton University, the Princeton Theological Seminary in New Jersey in 1828. Whereas, in Cincinnati, Ohio, a violent white mob drove out of the city, half of the African American residents dispite the progress of African Americans. However, for more than a century, white violence against northern African American urban communities has persisted.

The Oblate Sisters of Providence in Baltimore, Maryland, is founded. The first catholic order of black nuns in the United States was established in 1829.

The population of the United States in 1830 was 12, 866, 020 residents with a black population of 2, 328, 842, including 319, 599 free African Americans.

The first National Negro Convention was formed by African American delegates from New York, Pennsylvania, Maryland, Delaware, and Virginia and met in Philadelphia in 1830, to devise ways to challenge slavery in the South and racial discrimination in the North.

1831 had brought about many changes in slavery laws, North Carolina banned the teaching of slaves to read and write. Nat Turner leads a slave revolt in Southhampton, Virginia killing at least 57 whites and was hanged. Meanwhile, Alabama makes it illegal for blacks free or slave to preach the word of God. Moreover, in Pennsylvania, Jarena Lee's "The Life and Religious Experience of Jarena Lee, A Coloured Lady", the first autobiography written by a black woman.

We can not forget the "Trail of Tears" of 1831, when the Native Americans and their black slaves were driven out of Georgia, North Carolina, Alabama, Mississippi, Tennessee, and Florida to their new homes in the Indian Territory.

Although, change came slowly, but in 1832, Oberlin College was founded in Ohio. The college admitted African American men and women, and also white women for formal higher learning. Massachusetts in 1832, the first Female Anti-Slavery Society was founded, and was the first African American women society to protest slavery. Also that year, white philanthropists from Savannah,

Georgia established the first hospital dedicated specially to the care of African Americans.

Moreover, in1834, New York state incorporated the free black schools into the public school system.

Henry Blair, a free black farmer from Maryland, invented and received a U. S. patent for the mechanical corn planter in 1834. The machine dug the holes and planted the corn seed in the ground. That year in New York, David Ruggles, a black abolition activist, open the first black book store in New York City.

On March 2, 1836, the General Council of Texas declares independence from Mexico, and its Constitution, as an independent nation, recognizes slavery and make life difficult for the free blacks to remain. And on, March 6, the Alamo is captured by the Mexican Army led by General Lopez de Santa Ana. Hundreds of slaves leave the farms, and plantation to join or support the Mexican Army, but more took advantage of the war to escape south across the Rio Grand, or North across the Red River to Indian Territory. However, on April 22, General Santa Ana surrenders to General Sam Houston.

Meanwhile, other voices began to be raised against the evils of slavery, when the "In Supremo Apostolalus, " an apostolic letter written by Pope Gregory XVI in 1839, condemns the slave trade as the "inhuman traffic in Negroes, " but many U. S. Bishops as well as the men and women of the various religious orders owned slaves, and sometimes advocated for proper treatment. Bishop John England of Charleston, South Carolina, defends the slave trade saying, "it is a question for the Legislature and not for me". Whereas, on August 29th , American vessels tow the Spanish ship Armistad to port in New London, Connecticut with 53 slaves on board. The U. S, Supreme Court on March 9, 1841, freed the slaves, and returned them to Africa.

The U. S. census in 1840, showed 17, 069, 453 residents with a black population of 2, 873, 648, including 386, 293 free African Americans.

In New Orleans, Louisiana in 1842, Henrietta Delille, and Juliette Gaudin established the Catholic Sisters of the Holy Family, the second religious order for black women in the United States. The founders were biracial, and African decent. These were free women of color, a separate class and culture above the slave. The order ministered to poor black, educating them, and tending the sick.

However, in New York, in 1843, Sojourner Truth, and William Wells Brown began their campaign against slavery. Rev Henry Highland Garnett made his "Address to the Slaves", which ask for servile insurrection.

Meanwhile, on June 25, 1844, the Oregon State Legislative Committee of the Provisional Government enforced the first series of Black Exclusive Laws, which banned slavery and required slave-owners to free their slaves, but the African American that remained in Oregon after their freedom would be whip-lashed and expelled. That summer, George Bush, of African and Irish ancestry, set out for Oregon with his family, friends and neighbors, to escape prejudice in the slave state of Missouri. When they arrived in Oregon, they learned of the "Black Exclusion Law" , and traveled north to the north side of the Columbia River, which is now Washington state. On October, 1845, Bush established the town of "New Market", which was changed to Tumwater.

In 1845, Texas was annexed to the United States, and Congress declared war on Mexico in 1846.

Whereas, in 1847, Missouri banned the education of free African Americans, and the Dred Scott fight for freedom began. The decision wouldn't be handed down for another ten years. The state of Illinois, that year, had the first African American graduate from a U. S. medical school, Rush Medical College in Chicago, 1847.

His name was Dr. David Jones Peck.

When Brigham Young started his journey to the Salt Lake Valley in 1847. He was accompanied by three free African American pioneers, Green Flake, Oscar Crosby, and Hank Lay.

William Alexander Leidesdorff, an African American, sailed his 106 ton schooner around Cape Horn to California arriving in Verba Buena village (San Francisco) in 1841and was elected to the town council in 1847. He also became the town treasurer in 1848. However, a Missouri slave, Hiram Young, purchased his freedom, settled in Independence, Missouri, and became a yoke and wagon maker for the travelers on the Oregon and Santa Fe Trails.

Our country's western expansion exploded, when on February 2, 1848, Mexico and the United States signed the "Treaty of Guadalupe Hidalgo", transferring control of California, Arizona, New Mexico, Nevada, and Utah to the United States, and Mexico relinquished its claim of Texas for $20 million. That summer, the first Women Rights Convention was held in Seneca Falls, New York with Frederick Douglass in attendance.

The California Gold Rush began in 1849, with a least four thousand African Americans migrated to California. Moreover, in Maryland, Harriett Tubman, an escaped slave started her rescue efforts through the Underground Railroad. Back in San Francisco, California, early African American settlers started the first West Indian Benevolent Association, and the Mutual Benefit, and Relief Society for African Americans.

The census of 1850 in the United States showed a population of 23, 191, 876 residents with a black population of 3, 191, 876, including 433, 807 free African Americans.

The Compromise of 1850 allowed California, which was a free state that had more than 1, 000 slave, to enter the Union as a free state, but New Mexico, Utah would reserve their decision until later. Unforturnately, the Compromise also made it possible for stricter Fugitive Slave Laws. California being a free state had more than 1, 000 slaves, at that time. Although, there were more promising signs in 1850. For example, on August 27th , Lucy Stanton of Cleveland, Ohio was the first African American woman to graduate from college by completing all requirements at Oberlin Collegiate Institute ( now Oberlin College), but she did not receive a degree. In New York, the first black labor union is formed "The American League of Colored Workers". Harriett Tubman, an escape slave who had started her res-cue efforts in1849, led many enslaved African Americans in an escape through the Underground Railroad. She guided her parents, siblings, and 60 others to freedom. In December, 1851, she led 11 fugitives northward to freedom via the home of Frederick Douglass. During the Civil War, she worked as a cook and nurse for the Union Army.

She also became an armed scout and spy for the Union. Harriett led an armed expedition in the war, and guided the Combahee River Raid, which freed more than 700 slaves in South Carolina.

The state of California in 1851, began its first defense of the Fugitive Slave Law by defending a slave named Frank, and preventing him from being returned to enslavement. In Sacramento, St. Andrews African Methodist Episcopal Church was established, and was the first African American church west of Texas.

Moreover, in The City by the Bay, San Francisco, California, had an African American population of 464, the largest black population in the far west. Sacramento had the second largest had 338 African Americans, the second largest black population in California.

Although, the largest black owned businesses in 1852 San Francisco were the New England Soap Factory, owned by James P. Dyer, and the Pioneer Boot and Shoe Emporium, owned by Mifflin Gibbs and Peter Lester.

Also, Harriett Beecher Stowe published her book "Uncle Tom's Cabin", which not only becomes a best seller, but is a major influence in the Anti-Slavery Movement in New York.

Also in New York, Elizabeth Taylor Greenfield (The Black Swan) made her debuts at the Metropolitan Opera in 1853 and performed before Queen Victoria at Buckingham Palace in 1854. Meanwhile, in Utah, in 1852, Brigham Young, leader of the Church of Latter Day Saints began to preach the "Curse of Cain" doctrine, which he used to justify denial of African American males into the priesthood, even though, African Americans were among the first to convert to the Mormon faith.

Elijah Abel, an African American Mormon pioneer, settled in Salt Lake City in1853. He was an associate of Joesph Smith, was ordained to the LDS Mechizedek priesthood. Abel and his sons were the last African Americans to hold the office of priesthood in the church for 128 years.

And on May 24, 1854, a Virginia run away slave was captured in Boston and returned to slavery under the Fugitive Slave Law. Fifty thousand Bostonians watched as the slave, Anthony Burns, was paraded through the Boston streets in shackles. A Boston church raised $1, 500 to buy Burn's freedom. Burns eventually was freed and returned to Boston.

The issue of slavery became central to American policies in the mid 1800. Whereby, in Jackson, Michigan was the birth place of the Republican Party in 1854. It was formed in opposition to slavery in the western territories. However, on October 13th, Amun Institute is founded, and it was the first institution of higher learning for young African American men. The institution was established in Pennsylvania by John Miller Dickey, and his wife Sarah Emlen Cresson. And in Maine, 1854, James Augustine Healy, became the first black Jesuit priest in the catholic church, although he was ordained in France. He also became Bishop of Portland, Maine in 1875, a diocese that included all of Maine, and New Hampshire. Bishop Healy held the post for 25 years.

Whereas, in 1855, Massachusetts integrated all schools, and William C. Nell of Boston published the "Colored Patriots of the American Revolution. "This was the first African American history book. Moreover, Frederick Douglass was nominated by the Liberty Party of New York for the office of secretary of state.

On January 19, 1856, Bridget "Biddy" Mason, who was a slave in the free state of California, petitioned the court of California for her freedom after being enslaved for five years in the state, and she won her freedom. The Los Angeles District Judge Benjamin Hayes handed down the ruling in favor of Biddy and her family, citing California's 1850 constitution which prohibited slavery.

Wilberforce University in Ohio, becomes the first school of learning owned and operated by African Americans in 1856. It was founded by Bishop Daniel A. Payne of the A. M. E. church, and is the institution's first president.

The United States Supreme Court handed down the Dred Scott Decision on March 6, 1857, which the Supreme Court held that Scott was not free based on his residence in either Illinois or Wisconsin because he was not considered a person under the U. S. Constitution. However, in the opinion of the Supreme Court Justices, black people were not considered citizens when the Constitution was drafted in 1787.

Moreover, in 1858, Arkansas enforces their law to enslave all free African Americans who refuse to leave the state.

Civil resistance occurred, when on October 16, 1859, John Brown led 20 men, including five African Americans (John Copeland, Shields Green, Lewis S. Leary, Dangerfield Newby, and Osborne Anderson) in an unsuccessful raid on the Federal Armory at Harper's Ferry, Virginia (which is now West Virginia).

As we close the year 1859, our country is beginning to approach a period of unrest over economics and slavery with the African American caught in the middle. Life for the slave was very brutal for the most part, and racial discrimination for the free African Americans in North was escalating.

# CHAPTER 3

# LET FREEDOM RING

T he United States census taken in 1860 revealed a population explosion with 31,443, 321 residents with a black population of 4,441,830, including 488,070 free African Americans in the eastern states, and in the western territories, Texas has 182,556 black slaves and 355 free African Americans. There are counties in Texas that have more slaves than free African Americans, and whites. The Indian Territory has at least 7,000 African slaves making up 14 percent of the territories population.

The year 1861 ushered in state' secession from the Union, destruction, and war over economics and slavery for the South. However, on March 4, 1861, the Confederate States of America was formed in Texas. At the beginning of the Civil War, 200,000 blacks (most escaped or freed slaves) enlisted to serve in the Union Army and over 20,000 were killed in combat. And in the Indian Territory, the tribes were also divided with the Cherokees, Creeks, and Seminoles supporting the Union. And in October, the Cherokee and Creek united to form Union regiments and welcomed black men to join. Together, they formed the First Indian Home Guard, with 25 percent of the regiment African American. April 16, 1861,

Congress abolished slavery in the District of Columbia. Moreover, on December 20th , South Carolina was the first state to secede from the Union.

However, on May 12, 1862, a slave named Robert Smalls and seven other slaves commandeered a Confederate war vessel, escaped South Carolina harbor and sailed past Fort Sumter unseen to the Atlantic Ocean. There Smalls raised the white flag of surrender to the Union Navy. And in June, 1862, Congress abolished slavery in the western territories, and in July, Congress permitted African Americans to enlist in the U.S. Army, also established diplomatic relations with Haiti and Liberia, both black nations.

Moreover, Helena, in the Montana Territory, the first Anglo settlement in the West, was established after the discovery of gold in August, 1862, and black families were among the first residents of Helena. However, in Washington, D.C. in September, 1862, President Abraham Lincoln wrote the "Emancipation Proclamation" and declared that it would go in effect on July 1, 1863, providing the slave states had not returned to the Union by that time. And in Ohio, 1862, Mary Jane Patterson was the first African American woman to receive a Bachelor of Arts degree from Oberlin College. If you can recall, 12 years earlier, Lucy Stanton Day Sessions finished the requirements, but didn't receive a degree. Now, out west at Fort Lincoln, Kansas in 1862, the first Kansas Colored Infantry Regiment was formed on October, 17th in Bourbon County, Kansas. Meanwhile, in November, Leland Stanford became the first Republican Governor of California, but while in office, Governor Stanford and the Republican dominated Legislature began repealing many racially discrimination laws directed at the state's African Americans.

The Emancipation Proclamation finally went into effect throughout the United States on January 1, 1863, legally freeing all slaves. On February 21st , the Cherokee Indian Nation issued their Emancipation Proclamation abolishing slavery in the Indian Nation. The Cherokee Indian Nation was the only Indian Nation to abolish slavery before 1865. Whereas, on April 1, 1863, in San Francisco, California, Charlotte L. Brown, a black woman, was removed from a San Francisco street car by force, because of her race. Her father, who owned a livery stable, filed a law suit, on her behalf, against the street car company and won. And in Massachusetts, the 54th Massachusetts Volunteers was officially commissioned as an all black military unit of the U.S. Army on July 18th , however, on July, 17th , the first Kansas Colored Infantry with the Cherokee Indians and the white Colorado Union regiment defeated the Confederate forces at the battle of Honey Springs in Oklahoma. The battle was the largest in Indian Territory during the war. Meanwhile, Robert Smalls, the slave who had stolen a Confederate war ship, became the first and only black man commissioned a captain in the United States Navy during the Civil War. Also, in Savannah, Georgia, a lady named Susie King Taylor became the first black Army nurse in our country's history. African Americans continued to unite, when in Kansas, on October, 1863, 23 delegates representing 7,000 black Kansans gathered together in Leavenworth to form the first Kansas State Colored Convention.

African Americans' thirst for advancement was strong when in June, 1864, Rebecca Lee Crumler of Boston, became the first African American woman to earn a medical degree graduating from the New England Female Medical College in Boston, Massachusetts. Moreover, there was also good news for the black soldiers. When on June 15, 1864, the U.S Congress passed a bill giving equal pay, equipment, arms, and health care for black troops in the Union Army. However, in New Orleans, Louisiana, on October 4th , the La Tribune de la Nouvelle Orleans, which was renamed the New Orleans Tribune, was the first black-owned daily newspaper started publication.

General William T. Sherman issued Special Field Order #15 in January, 1865 that gave 400,000 acres of abandoned coastal land in the states of South Carolina, Georgia, and Florida to former slaves, whereby, the basis for the "40 acres and a mule". However, on February 1st, President Lincoln signed the 13th Amendment to the U.S. Constitution. This banned slavery throughout the United States, and on March 3rd, Congress established the Freedman's Bureau to provide health care, education, and technical assistance to emancipated slaves, although, in Texas, on June 19th , black people finally received news of their freedom. This event was celebrated each June, even today, by most black Americans and called Juneteenth Day. Whereas, in Houston, Texas, former slaves from central and east Texas gathered in one area in the city as the center of African American urban community called "Freedmantown" later renamed the Fourth Ward. Also, in the cities of Dallas, San Antonio, and Austin, the African Americans also formed urban communities. Moreover, the black people in Nevada came together from the towns of Virginia City, Gold Hill, and Silver City to form the Nevada Executive Committee to petition the state for the right to vote. However, 20,000 African American troops were among the 32,000 U.S. Army soldiers sent to the Rio Grande in Mexico, as a show of force against Emperor Maximilian's French troops, and some discharged black troops joined the forces of Benito Juarez, the Mexican Resistance leader. There were also some serious setbacks for the African American, between September and November of 1865, the "Jim Crow" legislation was born in the South and, the so called "Black Codes", were certain codes that African Americans must follow. Whereas, on December 24th , in Pulaski, Tennessee, the Ku Klux Klan was formed by six educated, middle class former Confederate veterans. They adopted terror tactics to destroy the aspirations of the African Americans and their supporters. Meanwhile, in Washington, D.C., President Lincoln, in 1865, appointed Captain Martin R. Delany to Major in the U.S. Army, making him the highest ranking black officer during the Civil War.

Meanwhile, on January 9, 1866, Fisk University opened its doors in Nashville, Tennessee, and was another stride toward African American educational advancement. Although, Andrew Johnson was elected President after Abraham Lincoln's death, on April 9th , the U.S. Congress overrode President Johnson's veto to enact the "Civil Rights Act of 1866". This would give citizenship to all black Americans and guaranteed equal rights with whites. This Civil Rights Act created turmoil in the country, for example in Memphis, Tennessee from May 1st thru the 3rd , white residents and Memphis police killed 46 black Americans and injured many more. They burned 90 black homes, 12 schools, and four churches in what came to be known as the "Memphis Massacre". However, on June 13th , the U.S. Congress approved the Fourteenth Amendment to the Constitution. The Amendment guaranteed due process and protection under the law to all citizens, and also gave citizenship to African Americans. It is amazing to realize it took from 1775 to 1866, and two amendments to the constitution for African Americans to become citizens of the country they help build. Also, Congress created four all-black regiments in the U.S. Army in the western territories. They were the 9th and 10th cavalry units and the 24th and 25th Infantry units. These became the first and only units of black soldiers to serve in the U.S. Army until the Spanish-American War. These regiments were know as "Buffalo Soldiers". Meanwhile, in Houston, Texas, the Antioch Missionary Baptist Church was founded and is the oldest continually operating African American church in Houston. Reverend John Henry Yates was chosen as the first pastor. However, more police violence occurred, in New Orleans, when the New Orleans police department, supporting the Democratic Mayor, raided a Republican meeting of blacks and whites on July 30th . The police killed 34 blacks and 3 white Republicans, with over 150 other people injured in the attack. Although, in November, Mifflin W. Gibbs was elected to the city council of Victoria, British Columbia, and became only the second black American elected to public office in North America. The first was John Mercer Langston, an African American lawyer elected to a congressional seat in Virginia. Whereas, Cathay Williams became the first African American woman to join the Union Army. She was born a slave of a free black father, and a slave mother. She grew up working for the Union Army as a cook, laundress and nurse. She was a very adventurous woman, but, while in Arkansas, she saw African American men in Union uniforms. Moreover, she wanted to be a soldier, because she was tired of cooking, and washing clothes. She changed her name to William Cathay, and enlisted in the U.S. Army on November 15th . She served about four years in the 38th Infantry, as a Buffalo Soldiers.

However, a veto by President Andrew Johnson was over turned by Congress, on January 8, 1867, but, Congress granted black citizens of the District of Columbia the right to vote. Two days later, Congress passed the "Territorial Suffrage Act" allowing black Americans in the western territories the right to vote. In Atlanta, Georgia, on February 14th , Morehouse College, an all black college, was established to further their education. Whereas, on March 2nd , the Reconstruction Act was signed, which enfranchised the former slaves in the south. Also, in Washington, D.C., Congress chartered Howard University, whicht he institution was named after General Oliver O. Howard, who headed the Freedman's Bureau. On July 4th , in Houston, Texas, 140 African Americans and 20 whites met to form the Texas Republican Party. The first chairman was Elisha M. Pease.

# CHAPTER 4

# FREEDOM

T he census of 1860 revealed a growth explosion of a population of 31,443,321 residents and a black population of 4,441,830, including 488,070 free African Americans in the East. In the western territories, Texas had 182,556 black slaves, and 355 free African Americans. There were counties in Texas that had more slaves than free people. The Indian Territories had at least 7,000 black slaves making up 14 percent of the territory's population.

The coming years brought secession which split the Union, and eventually caused war between the states because of slavery and economics in the South. On November 6, 1860, Abraham Lincoln was elected President of the United States. And, on December 20, South Carolina was the first state to secede from the Union.

Moreover, in February, 1861, Mississippi, Florida, Alabama, Louisiana, and Texas also seceded from the Union and formed the Confederate States of America. The United States Congress immediately passed the very first Confiscation Act which stopped Confederate slave owners from enslaving runaways. And on May 2, 1861, the black men of New Orleans, Louisiana organized the First Louisiana Native Guard of the Confederate Army. The Guard was the first and only military unit of black officers and enlisted men to fight for the South. On February, 1862, after the Union occupation of New Orleans, the Guard became a military unit in the United States Army. However, during the Civil War approximately 200,00 blacks (mostly newly escaped/free slaves) served in the Union Army, and over 20,000 were killed in combat. And, in October, 1861, in Indian Territory, the Cherokee and Creek Nations united to form Union regiments, which welcomed black men to join. This resulted in the First Indian Home Guard being formed, and by 1864, 25 percent of the regiment was African American.

United States Congress abolished slavery in the District of Columbia on April 16, 1862, and in the following month in Charleston, South Carolina, Robert Smalls and seven other slaves commandeered a Confederate battleship and escaped Charleston harbor. They sailed past Fort Sumter to the Atlantic Ocean undetected, where he raised a white flag, and surrendered to the Union Navy.

However, in June, Congress abolished slavery in the western territories. And on July 17th , Congress permitted blacks to enlist in the U.S. Army. Also, Congress established diplomatic relations with two black nations, Haiti and Liberia. `Whereas, in August, out West, after the discovery of gold in Montana Territory, the town of Helena was established and among the first residents were several black families. And in September, President Lincoln wrote the Emancipation Proclamation that freed all slaves, however, he declared that it would go into effect on July 1, 1863, if the slave states haven't returned to the Union. Meanwhile, in Ohio, Mary Jane Patterson became the first African American to receive a B.A. degree from Oberlin College, whereas, 12 years earlier, Lucy Stanton Day Sessions completed the requirements for a degree, but wasn't awarded a degree. However, on October 17th , in Bourbon County, at Fort Lincoln, Kansas, the first Kansas Colored Infantry Regiment was formed. And in California, in November, Leland Stanford became the first Republican governor, while in office with the help of the dominate Republican legislature repealed many racially discriminating laws directed at the blacks in the state.

The Emancipation Proclamation finally takes effect through-out the United States on January 1, 1863, legally freeing all slaves. Whereas, on February 21st , in Indian Territory, the Cherokee Indian Nation issued their Emancipation Proclamation abolishing slavery in the Cherokee Nation and were the only Indian Nation to abolish slavery before 1865. And on April 17th , in San Francisco, California, Charlotte L. Brown, a black woman, was forcibly removed from a street car because of her race. However, her father, a livery stable owner, filed a lawsuit against the street car company and won. Whereas, in Oklahoma, on July 17th , at the Battle of Honey Springs, the Kansas Colored Infantry of blacks and Cherokee Indians with the white Colorado Union Regiments defeated Confederate troops, on July 17th, and was the largest military battle in Indian Territory during the Civil War. Also, on July 18th , the 54th Massachusetts Volunteers was officially commissioned an all black military unit in the United States Army. And in Washington, D.C., Robert Smalls, an escaped slave from South Carolina, became the first and only African American commissioned a captain in the United States Navy during the Civil War. However, in Savannah, Georgia, Susie King Taylor became the first black Army nurse in history.

Meanwhile, in Kansas, in October, 1863, 23 delegates repre-senting 7,000 black Kansans gather in Leavenworth to form the first Kansas State Colored Convention.

Through the horrors of war, a bright light shone in June, 1864, when Dr. Rebecca Lee Crumpler of Boston, became the first African American woman to earn a medical degree in the United States. She graduated from the New England Female Medical College in Boston. And on June 15th , the U.S. Congress passed a bill giving equal pay, equipment, arms and health care for black troops in the Union Army. And in Louisiana, on October 4th , the La Tribune de la Nouvelle Orleans (the New Orleans Tribune) became the first black owned daily newspaper published in Louisiana.

However, in January, 1865, General William T. Sherman issued Special Field Order #15, giving 400,000acres of abandon coastal land in the states of South Carolina, Georgia, and Florida to for-mer slaves. The Special Field Order was the basis for the "40 acres and a mule". And President Abraham Lincoln, on February 1, 1865, signed the 13th Amendment to the Constitution banning slavery throughout the United States, also, on March 3rd , Congress established the Freedmen Bureau which provided health care, education and technical assistance to emancipated slaves. Moreover, in Texas, on June 19th , the black slaves finally received news of their emancipation and declared that day "Juneteenth Day" which is still celebrated. Because of the signing, during the summer, former slaves from central and east Texas gathered in a section of Houston to form "Freedmantown", and became the center for African American urban community. The black section of Houston would later be renamed Fourth Ward. The cities of Dallas, San Antonio and Austin would also have their black urban communities. And in Nevada, the black men from Virginia City, Gold Hill and Silver City gathered to form the Nevada Executive Committee to petition the state for the right to vote. However, in Mexico, 20,000 black troops were among the 32,000 soldiers sent to the Rio Grande as a show of force against Emperor Maximilian's French troops. Meanwhile, some discharged black soldiers joined the forces of Benito Juarez, the Mexican Resistance leader in opposing the French troops. Furthermore, between September and November, the "Jim Crow" legislation was born which initiated the so called "Black Codes". Thus, in Pulaski, Tennessee, on December, 24th , the Ku Klux Klan was formed by six educated, middle class former Confederate veterans. They adopted terror tactics to destroy the aspirations of the black Americans and their white supporters. Meanwhile, in Washington, D.C., President Lincoln appointed Captain Martin R. Delany to the rank of Major which made him the highest ranking black officer in the U.S. Army during the Civil War.

On January 9, 1866, Fisk University, in Nashville, Tennessee was founded. And on April 9th , the U.S. Congress overrode President Andrew Johnson's veto to enact the Civil Rights Act which would give citizenship to black Americans and guarantee equal rights with whites. However, in Memphis, Tennessee, during May 1st thru 3rd , white residents and police killed 46 black Americans and injuring many more, also they burned 90 homes, destroyed 12 schools and four churches. The incident was known as the Memphis Massacre. Meanwhile, in Washington, D.C., on June 13th , Congress approved the 14th Amendment to the Constitution which guaranteed due process and equal protection under the law to all citizens and enforces the citizenship for African Americans. Incredibly, citizenship for the African American took from 1775 to 1866 and two Amendments to the Constitution for the people that helped build this Nation from scratch. During this session, Congress also created four all black regiments in the U.S. Army and they were the 9th and 10th cavalry and the 24th and 25th Infantry units. They were the first and only black soldiers in the U.S. Army to serve in West until the Spanish-American War and these units were known as the "Buffalo Soldiers". Moreover, in Houston, Texas, the Antioch Missionary Baptist Church was founded and Reverend John Henry Yates became the first pastor, also the church is the oldest continually operating black church in the city. Meanwhile, on July 30, 1866, in New Orleans, Louisiana, the police supporting the Democratic major raided a Republican meeting of black and white people killing 34 black and 3 white people also injuring 150 others in the attack. However, in November, in Victoria, British Columbia, Mifflin W. Gibbs was elected to the city council and he became only the second black American elected to public office in North America. The first was John Mercer Langston who was elected to the office of city clerk in Ohio.

On January 8, 1867, President Andrew Johnson's veto was overrode by Congress granting the black citizens of the District of Columbia the right to vote. And two days, Congress passed the "Territorial Suffrage Act" allowing the black citizens in the Western Territories the right to vote. Meanwhile, on February 14th , in Atlanta, Georgia, Morehouse College was founded. And on March 2nd , the Reconstruction Act was signed dividing ten of the eleven ex- Confederate states into military districts, also reorganizing post-war Southern governments and disenfranchising former high ranking Confederates also, enfranchising former slaves in the South. That same day in Washington, D.C., Howard University, which was named after General Oliver O. Howard the head of the Freedman's Bureau, was chartered by Congress. However, on July 4th , 140 black and 20 white men meet in Houston, Texas to form the Texas Republican Party and elected Elisha M. Pease as the first chairman.

However, on July 21, 1868, the 14th Amendment to the Constitution was ratified granting citizenship to any person born or naturalized in the United States. And in Opelousas, Louisiana, on September 28th , approximately, 200 to 300 black citizens were killed by white mobs opposing the Reconstruction Act and black voting.

Meanwhile, in November, General Ulysses S. Grant was elected President of the United States. And in Louisiana, John Willis Menard became the first black elected to Congress from Louisiana Second Congressional District. However, neither Menard or his opponent would obtain the seat because of election disputes. Whereas, in Texas, the era of the cattle drive began with William G. Butler who organized a cattle drive using black and latino cowboys. And for the next two decades, black cowboys would participate in many trail drives from central Texas to the rail heads in Abilene and Dodge City, Kansas, Denver, Colorado, and Cheyenne, Wyoming. Also, on November 9th , in Washington, D.C., Howard University Medical School opened and was the first medical school established for the training of black doctors in the United States.

On February 26, 1869, Congress sent the 15th Amendment to the Constitution to the states for approval which guaranteed black males the right to vote throughout the United States, also, in Wyoming black women obtained the right to vote. And on April 6th , President Grant appointed Ebenezer Don Carlos Bassett Ambassador to Haiti and the first black diplomat of the United States. Moreover, in Massachusetts, George Lewis Rufflin became the first black to graduate from Harvard Law School. Meanwhile, in Promontory, Utah, the transcontinental railroad was joined uniting the country. Once the railroad was completed approximately 300 black railroad workers migrated to Oakland, California and as the number of workers increased the Pullman Car Company requiring black male porters in each passenger rail car provided employment for the railroad workers. And in Fort Bend County, Texas, Walter Moses Burton was elected the first black sheriff in the western United States. Also, in Texas, in November, Matthew Gaines of Washington County and

George T. Ruby of Galveston became the first black men elected to the Texas State Senate.

By 1870 the population of the United States had grown enormously with a population of 39,818,449 residents including a black population of 4,880,009 and no slaves.

A noted change in attitude and a milestone for equal rights, when on February 25, 1870, Hiram R. Revels became the first black man elected State Senator of Mississippi. He replaced Jefferson Davis completing his unexpired term. However, on March 30th , the 15th Amendment to the Constitution was ratified and black men were allowed to vote. The 15th Amendment stated " the right of any citizen of the United States to vote shall not be denied or abridged by the United States or by any state on account of race, color, or previous condition of servitude." And in June, in Massachusetts, Richard T. Greener became the first black undergraduate to graduate from Harvard University. Also, on June 28th , Emanuel Stance, a 23 year old black soldier from F Troop, 9th Cavalry became the first Buffalo Soldier to win the Congressional Medal of Honor. Whereas, in Washington, D.C. Dunbar High School was opened, but was first named the Preparatory High School for Colored Youth. And in Travis County, Texas, Bill Pickett, the most famous black cowboy performer, was born. As a rodeo cowboy, in invented a way to control steers by bulldogging, as it was called which made him a star attraction in wild west shows.

However, in February, 1871, Congress passed the third Civil Rights Act which was known as the Ku Klux Klan Act. This Act dismantled the KKK until the 20th Century.

Moreover, in 1871, the spirit of freedom and equality within our nation was illustrated, when George Washington, an early black settler of Washington State, founded a predominately white town called Centerville, which is now known as Centralia, Washington. And in Nashville, Tennessee, on October 6, 1871, on the campus of Fisk University, the Jubilee Singers was founded, a choral group singing black gospel spirituals, who has performed before the Queen of England and the Emperor of Japan.

However, in Louisiana, in 1872, Lt Governor Pinckney Benton Stewart Pinchback was elected governor for one month from December, 1872 to January, 1873, because to incumbent governor was impeached. And in Washington, D.C., Charlotte Ray became the first black woman attorney accepted to the bar in D.C. and permitted to practice law in the United States. Also, on a plantation in Tennessee, Nat Love, the famous black cowboy, was born to a free black father and slave mother, learned to break horses at an early age on the plantation, and at 16 years old left the plantation and went west. He got a job with the Duval Ranch of Texas as a ranch hand. There he learned and perfected his skills as a ranch hand. He also became very proficient with the use of the .45 revolver. He went to Arizona, after three years earned a reputation as a all around cowboy earning the nickname of "Red River Dick". On a cattle drive to Deadwood, South Dakota, he won $200 in an all-around cowboy competition earning the nickname of "Deadwood Dick".

When the 43rd Congress convened in 1873, there was only seven black congressional members. Also in Washington, D.C., Bishop Patrick Healy, a black Roman Catholic Bishop, became president of Georgetown University from 1873 to 1881 and became the first black to preside over a predominately white university, by the way, nobody knew he was black. But, on February 23rd , in Tennessee, the "Jim Crow Laws" were enacted. These laws were similar to the existing laws in the North prior to the Civil War. However, on Easter Sunday, in Colfax, Louisiana over 100 blacks were killed in this northeastern Louisiana town defending the black Republicans in local office against white militia and today the incident is known as the Colfax Massacre.

Meanwhile, when Congress convened in 1875 there was only eight black members. And on March 1, 1875, enacted the Civil Rights Act which gave all black Americans the right to public accomodation and jury duty. And on March 3rd , in Mississippi, Blanche Kelso Bruce became the first black to serve a full six year term in the United States Senate. When the Kentucky Derby was established on May 17th , it was first held at the Louisville Jockey Club, now Churchill Downs. The first winning jockey was Oliver Lewis, a black man, who rode a horse named Aristide and won. And over the next 27 years, 14 black jockeys would win the Kentucky Derby.

However, in Boston, Massachusetts, on March 7, 1876, Lewis H. Latimar, a black inventor and draftsman, worked for a patent attorney office and was hired to assist Alexander Graham Bell to draft plans to obtain a patent for the telephone. And in May, in Connecticut, Edward Alexander Bouchet received a PHD in Physics from Yale University, and was the first black to receive a Doctorate Degree from any American university, but he was never permitted to do any research or work in physics because of his race. Meanwhile, during the summer, race riots and terrorism erupted against black voters in South Carolina including the "Hamburg Massacre, where many blacks were killed celebrating the 4th of July, and President Grant sent troops to restore order. Although, in Nashville, Tennessee, on October 13th , the Meharry Medical College was founded by the Freedman's Aid Society of the Methodist Church.

In Washington, D.C., in 1877, Rutherford B. Hayes was elected President of the United States which put an end to the Reconstruction Era, also ended federal efforts to protect the civil rights of black Americans, and when the 45th Congress convened there was only 3 black congressional members seated. But, on June 15th , at the U.S. Military Academy in West Point, New York, Lt Henry O. Flipper became the first black man to graduate from the Academy followed by John Hanks Alexander in 1887 and Charles Young in 1889. Lt Flipper black officer to command a troop of Buffalo Soldiers in the 10th Calvary at Fort Concho, Texas. Meanwhile, on July 30th , 30 black families from Kentucky led by W.H. Smith, Benjamin Carr and four other black men established the town of Nicodemus, an agricultural colony, in western Kansas and was one of many all black towns to spring up in the West.

# CHAPTER 5

# THE FIGHT FOR
# REAL FREEDOM

O ur journey continues through the 20th Century with the end of slavery. The Emancipation Proclamation removed the physical chains of slavery, but still we were slaves to hatred, discrimination, degradation, and denial of equal rights. Come travel with me to see how we, as a people, become deeply involved in the growth of our Nation.

The Census of the United States in 1900 revealed a population of 75,994,575 residents, including a black population of 8,833,994 residents.

In January, 1900, James Weldon Johnson, and his brother John, wrote the lyrics, and composed the music for "Lift Every Voice and Sing" in Jacksonville, Florida. The song was written to celebrate the birthday of Abraham Lincoln, and adopted as the Black National Anthem. And in New Orleans, Louisiana, a tragedy occurred on July 23, 1900, when an African American, Robert Charles and his roommate were sitting on a porch in a predominately white neighborhood, when they were harassed by two city policemen. One officer pulled his pistol, and began shooting then, Robert Charles pulled his pistol and fired back, fortunately, no one was injured. Charles ran away, and a manhunt ensued. The white citizens rioted for 4 days and killed 12 African Americans and 7 white were also killed. However, good news in Boston, Massachusetts, on August 23rd ,when Booker T. Washington founded the National Negro Business League. The League promoted African American business enterprise. A large West Indian immigration into the United States occurred at the beginning of 1900, and will continue for many years after. At that time, two-thirds of the landowners in the Mississippi Delta were black farmers and most of them brought and cleared their land after the Civil War, also, in Oklahoma, approximately, 8,000 African Americans acquired 1.5 million acres of land, as a result of the unsettled land in the Oklahoma Territory.

Also, during 1900, approximately, 30,000 black teachers were trained since the Civil War. These teachers assisted more than half of the black population to achieve literacy.

Whereas, out West, the Buffalo Soldiers were sent to Peking, China, as part of a U.S. military force to suppress the Boxer Rebellion, Another set back for the African Americans, when in North Carolina, George H. White, a Republican, is the last African American congressman elected to Congress in the 19th Century, and he leaves office in 1901. No African American will serve in Congress for the next 28 years.

However, on October 11, 1901, the first African American recording artists, Bert Williams, and George Walker, recorded "Her Name's Miss Dinah Fair" for the Victor Talking Machine Company(RCA Victor) in New York City. Meanwhile, in Washington, D.C., on October 16, President Theodore Roosevelt met with Booker T. Washington at the White House, and Washington was invited to dinner, which makes the Tuskegee educator, the first African American to dine at the White House. President Roosevelt's kind act started a national outrage. After leaving the Washington, D.C., Booker T. Washington returned to Tuskegee Institute to publish his autobiography "Up From Slavery".

Moveover, in Louisville, Kentucky, in May, 1902, jockey Jimmy Winkfield won the Kentucky Derby at the age of 19. He rode a horse called Eminence. He accomplished this, in an era,when African American jockeys dominated the sport.

W.E.B. Du Bois, on April 27, 1903, published his denouncement of gradualism advocated by Booker T. Washington, and called for agitation for African American rights. Also, in Los Angeles, California, the community of Watts was established, and it was a racially integrated suburban community consisting of blacks, whites, and latinos. During this period, African American women continued to make advancements, when Maggie Lena Walker chartered the St. Luke's Penny Savings Bank in Richmond, Virginia, and became the first African American female to charter, open, and operate a black bank in the United States. Moreover, Mary McLeod Bethune, an African American educator, established a school for African American girls in Daytona Beach, Florida in her quest to improve the educational standards of the African American, she merged her school with a private black boys school to form the Bethune-Cookman School, which was later named Bethune-Cookman University.

Dr. Solomon Carter Fuller, an African American from New York, trained in Psychiatric at the Royal Psychiatric Hospital, University of Munich in Germany, under Dr. Alois Alzheimer. Meanwhile, In 1904, he became widely known pioneer for his research of Alzheimer's disease, plus he is the nations first black psychiatrist. Although, in the west, the Kinkaid Homestead Act of 1904, allowed 200 black families to settle the Sand Hill district of north-central Nebraska. The settlers claimed 40,000 acres of land, and created the town of Dewitty, later renamed Audacious.

In Chicago, Illinois, on May 5, 1905, Robert Abbott established the Chicago Defender, a weekly black newspaper, which had the largest circulation of any black newspaper in the United States. And, on July 11th thru 13th , the Niagara Movement was formed by 29 black business owners, teachers, and clergy under the leadership of W.E.B. Du Bois, and William Monroe Trotter both gentlemen were civil rights activist. The Movement was organized in opposition to Booker T. Washington's Accomodationism. They drafted a Declaration of Principles, that stated "We refuse to allow the impression to remain that the Negro-American assents to inferiority, is submissive under oppression, and apologetic before insults."

Moreover,the beginning of the Pentecostal Movement was started at the Azusa Street Revival in Los Angeles, California in 1906. The Movement Revival was led by black evangelist, William J. Seymore. The Movement spread worldwide. However, in Brownsville, Texas, August 13, 1906, soldiers of the all-black 25th Infantry Unit of the U.S. Army, had been harassed by the city police, and discriminated against by the local citizens. A group of unidentified men fired at least a hundred shots throughout the city and a bartender was killed. The citizens accused the black soldiers of the incident. When the soldiers were question about who fired the shots, the soldiers had no answer. So, in retaliation, President Theodore Roosevelt, thinking the soldiers were hiding the person or persons, dishonorably discharged 167 soldiers. The soldiers were finally cleared of all charges during an investigation in 1970. The incident was known as the "Brownsville Affray". However, on the campus of Cornell University, on December 4th , seven African American students formed the Alpha Phi Alpha Fraternity, and was the first college fraternity for African American men in the United States.

A blessing for African American women, when Sarah Breedlove, A.K.A., Madame C.J. Walker of Denver, Colorado, in 1907, developed and marketed a hair straightening method, and hair products for black women. She created one of the most successful cosmetics companies for African Americans in the Nation. And in Philadelphia, Pennsylvania, Alain Locke, a Howard University graduate, became the first African American to receive a Rhodes Scholar. Meanwhile, across the state in Pittsburgh, Robert Vann, an African American, take control as editor-publisher of the Pittsburgh Couier. Although, in the West on November 16th , Indian Territory and Oklahoma were admitted into the Union as the state of Oklahoma, and immediately, the state legislature disenfranchised the black voters, segregated public schools and accomodations.

In Washington, D.C., on January 15 1908, on the campus of Howard University, the Alpha Kappa Alpha Sorority was founded is the first black sorority in the Nation. Also in sports, on December 26th, in Sydney, Australia, Jack Johnson of Galveston, Texas defeated Canadian Tommy Burns in a heavyweight title bout. He became the first African American heavyweight boxing champion of the world.

Meanwhile, on February 12, 1909, in New York City, the National Association for the Advancement of Colored People (NAACP) was formed in response to the Springfield, Illinois Riot, which 2 blacks and 4 whites were killed. Another milestone happened on April 6th, when Admiral Robert E. Peary, and his "first man" African American artic explorer, Matthew Henson, accompanied by four Inuit Native Americans became the first known men to reach the North Pole. However, in Mobile, Alabama, the Knights of Peter Claver was formed, and became the first national black catholic fraternal order. The Knights of Peter Claver was formed because black catholic men were not accepted into the Knights of Columbus. Meanwhile, speaking of sports, the first African American collegiate basketball teams were formed with the universities at Lincoln, Virginia Union, Hampton Institute, and Wilberforce University.

As we travel further into the 20th Century, the census of the population in the United States at the beginning of 1910 revealed 93,402,151 residents, including a black population of 9,827,763.

On September 29, 1910, the National Urban League was established in New York City. The League was formed to assist African Americans in obtaining employment, and adjusting to urban life style. Also, in New York City, on November 1st, W.E.B. Du Bois became the first editor of the official NAACP publication "Crisis". However, on December 19th, in Baltimore, Maryland, the city council approved an ordinance segregating black and white neighborhoods, also the following cities enacted similar ordinances: Dallas, Texas, Greenboro, North, Carolina, Louisville, Kentucky, Norfolk, Virginia, Oklahoma City, Oklahoma, Richmond, Virginia, and St. Louis, Missouri. Whereas, in Denver, Colorado, an African American couple, Oliver Toussaint Jackson, and his wife Minerva had a vision of building an all black town. They went through many trials and tribulations, being rejected, but finally, with help from the newly elected Governor of Colorado, they filed claim on 320 acres of land in Weld County, where they established the colony of Dearfield, Colorado. A town where African Americans could escape racism, discrimination, degradation.

Meanwhile, two fraternities for African American men were founded on U.S. campuses in 1911. The first was on the campus of the University of Indiana on January 5th , the Kappa Alpha Psi was established, and on November 17th on the campus of Howard University the Omega Psi Phi Fraternity was established.

# CHAPTER 6

# OPPORTUNITY KNOCKS

T he United States Census of 1930 showed a population of 122,775,046 residents including a black population of 11,891,143.

In 1930, in Detroit, Michigan, Wallace Ford Muhammad established the Black Muslim Movement. He preached the the recently migrated black from the South.

And in New York City, in 1931, Walter White was appointed the NAACP Executive Secretary. He initiated a plan of using lawsuits to end racial discrimination. However, on March 25, 1931, in Scottsboro, Alabama, nine black teenagers, known as the Scottsboro Boys, were arrested for the rape of two white women on a freight train. The case was submerged in racism, fabrications of accounts and denial of constitutional right to a fair trial. Prior to the indictment, the accusers were confronted with lynch mobs, a frame up of facts, an all white jury and a rush to a verdict. The boys were eventually sentenced to death, even though, medical evidence revealed no crime had been committed. Moreover, in Rochester, New York, William Grant Still became the first African American classical composer and conductor to have his music played by the New York Philharmonic

Orchestra. He conducted the orchestra in his presentation of "The Afro-American Symphony".

At Tuskegee Institute in 1932, the U.S. Public Health Service conducted the Tuskegee Syphillis Experiment. The Health Service under a pretense of free health care for African American men, injected 201 black men with syphillis. But, when the funding ran out the U.S. Health Service didn't tell the men that they had syphillis, nor tell them about a treatment. The experiment lasted until 1972. However, in Chicago, Illinois, gospel composer, Thomas Dorsey writes "Take My Hand Precious Lord", which has been a long time favorite with both black and white choirs, and churches.

Whereas, in Atlanta, Georgia, in 1934, Dr. W.E.B. Dubois vacated his position with the NAACP because of the advocacy of African American controlled institutions, school and economic cooperatives. This was against the NAACP campaign for integration advocated by Roy Wilkins, civil rights activist, who assumed Dr. Dubois position and editor of the "Crisis". Also, in Sacramento, California, the California State Assembly welcomed the newly elected, 27 year old African American Democratic, Augustus Hawkins to the Assembly. He will retain the seat for 32 years. And in New York City, the famous Apollo Theater opened in Harlem, where many talented black men and women were discovered.

However, in Harlem, on March 20, 1935, a one day riot erupted because of high unemployment and police brutality. The results of the riot was three blacks killed, at least sixty injured, and over $200 million in property damage. Meanwhile, in Washington, D.C., on April 1st , the U.S. Supreme Court ruled in the Norris V. Alabama case that a defendant has the right to trial bu jury of his or her peers. Moreover, the ruling wasn't followed in many states for a long time. And on November 5th , the Maryland Supreme Court ruled in the Murray V. Pearson case that the University of Maryland must admit blacks into their law school or establish a separate school for African Americans. The university choose to admit their first black student, Donald Gaines Murray, Sr. Whereas, in New York City, on December 24th , Mary Mcleod Bethune, founder of Bethune-Cookman University, gathered 28 national black women organization to form the National Council of Negro Women with a mission to advance the opportunities and quality of life for African American women, their families and communities, also a need to harness the power and extending the leadership of African American women through a national organization.

Moreover, in Chicago, Illinois, on February 14, 1936, the National Negro Congress held their first meeting and nearly 600 black organizations were represented. Whereas, another proud moment for African American women equality occurred, on June 24th , when Mary McLeod Bethune was named Director of the Negro Affairs Division of the National Youth

Administration, which makes her the highest ranking black official in President Roosevelt's administration. Also, she was the first black woman to receive a presidential appointment. But, in Dallas, Texas, political leader, Reverend Maynard H. Jackson, Sr. And Antonio Maceo Smith established the Progressive Citizens League, which was later renamed the Progressive Voters' League. The League attacked the restrictions on black voting rights, and became one of the most effective black political groups in Texas. However, in Massachusetts, Dr. William Augustus Hinton was the first black doctor to write and publish a medical textbook. His book is "Syphillis and Its Treatment." Meanwhile, at the Olympic Games in Berlin, Germany, on August 3rd thru 9th , African American track star, Jesse Owens competed in four events and won Gold Medals in each event.

President Roosevelt, on March 26, 1937, appointed William H. Hastie as Federal judge presiding of the Virgin Islands. He was the first black appointed to the federal bench.

# CHAPTER 7

# THE WINDS OF CHANGE

T he U.S. Census taken in 1940 revealed a population of 131,669,275 total residents, including a black population of 12,865,518.

The decade and year began in celebration, when on February 29, 1940, in Los Angeles, California, Hattie McDaniel received the Oscar award for the Best Supporting Actress in her role in the film "Gone With the Wind". She was the first black actor to receive an Academy Award. Also, Richard Wright, the literary novelist, published his first novel the "Native Son". Furthermore, in New York, Dr. Charles R. Drew, physician, surgeon, and medical researcher, presented his graduate thesis on Banked Blood. And, while at the Columbia-Presbyterian Medical Center, he discovered that plasma can replace whole blood transfusion. However, towards the end of 1940, Charles Hamilton Houston and Thurgood Marshall created the NAACP Legal Defense Fund, which was the leading civil rights organization in the United States, and the Legal Defense Fund was headquartered in New York City. And, Mary Lucinda Dawson was the leader of a movement to promote African American appreciation and participation in opera, so in 1941, she established the

National Negro Opera Company, in Pittsburgh, Pennsylvania. Also, Benjamin O. Davis, Sr. was the first African American to be promoted to the general officer rank in the U.S. Army. Now, in Alabama, the U.S. Army forms the Tuskegee Air Squadron at the Tuskegee Institute, and the squadron would be known as the "Tuskegee Airmen". Moreover, in Washington, D.C., President Franklin D. Roosevelt, on June 25, 1941, issued Executive Order 8802, which integrated war production plants, and established the Fair Employment Practice Committee (FEPC). This was in desperation for the need of factory workers to build the equipment required to win World War II, with a large migration of African Americans from the South and West to the Northern cities increased the labor force. The migration transformed U.S. politics as more blacks vote and afford new homes increased pressure on Congress to protect civil rights of African Americans throughout the Nation., But in Los Angeles, California, the Negro Victory Committee was formed by Reverend Clayton Russell, as a mass means of civil disobedience tactics to oppose racial discrimination. And sadly, tragedy strikes in the Pacific, when on December 7, 1941, the Japanese forces attacked Pearl Harbor, Hawaii, and during the attack, on the U.S. ship the West Virginia, Dorris "Dorrie" Miller distinguished himself with feats of bravery, and was awarded the Navy Cross for his heroism. While teaching at the Livingston College in North Carolina, Margaret Walker, the renown poet, and writer, published "For My People", a book of poems, which she used as for her Master's thesis at the University of Iowa. Moreover, in Chicago, Illinois, the Congress of Racial Equality (CORE) was created by African Americans James Farmer, Jr, George Houser, Bernice Fisher, James Russell Robinson, Joe Guinn, and Homer Jack. CORE's mission was to bring about equality for all people regardless, of race, creed, sex, age, disability, sexual orientation, religion, or ethnic background. Also, the U.S. Marine Corps accepted the first African American men, at any time period. They had separate training facilities at Camp Montford Point, North Carolina, and was known as the Montford Point Marines. Furthermore, at Fort Des Moines in Iowa, Charity

Adams Earley became the first black woman to be commissioned an officer in the Womens' Army Auxilliary Corps (WAAC). And in New York, Hugh Mulzac was the first African American to be commissioned captain in the American Merchant Marine. Also, in the sports world, baseball pitcher, Satchel Paige led the Kansas City Monarchs, of the Negro Baseball League, to their 4th Negro American League Baseball Championship. An example of Liberty, and Justice for All, was demonstrated in Los Angeles, when newspaper editor, Charlotta Bass, California Assemblyman, Augustus Hawkins, actresses Hattie McDaniel and Lena Horne, collaborated with the Citizens Committee for the Defense of Mexican American Youth, which was formed by actor Anthony Quinn and Josephine Fierro de Bright of the Spanish-Speaking People's Congress in the defense of eight Mexican-American men charged with the murder of Jose Diaz.

With war in Europe and in the Pacific, we find more violence on the home front in 1943, for example in Los Angeles, California, on June 3rd, the Zoot Suit Riots erupted, when white saliors, soldiers, and marines attacked local youths, consisting of African Americans and Mexican Americans, wearing zoot suits. The riots lasted four days, and only 9 sailors were arrested, however, several hundred zoot suiters were arrested, and some died of injuries in jail. And in Detroit, Michigan, New York City, Harlem, Mobile, Alabama, and Beaumont, Texas, on June 20th and 21st , riots erupted and at least 34 lives were lost, including 25 African Americans. However, there were military accomplishments that year, example, during the summer, at Fort Huachuca in Arizona, 14,000 black soldiers of the 93rd Infantry Division, and the 32nd and 33rd Companies of the Women Army Auxilliary Corps, approximately, 300 women, are assigned for training, and this was the largest concentration of black military personnel in U.S. history. Also, in Annapolis, Maryland, and all Naval Officer Schools, accepted African American men for the first time in United States history. And, how about this. We will never witness this again in history, when two U.S. Navy war ships were manned entirely by African Americans. They were the crews on the USS Mason, a Destroyer, and the PC1264, Submarine Chaser.

Moreover, in Alabama at the Tuskegee Institute, the 99th Pursuit Squadron, a unit of the Tuskegee Airmen, made their first combat mission in Italy. Whereas, in Denver, Colorado, the Congress of Racial Equality mounted their first successful protest demonstration in the West, when, they picketed a Denver movie theater, because of of segregation.

Another strike for equality, when on April 3, 1944, the U.S. Supreme Court ruled in the Smith V. Allwright case declared that the state of Texas "Whites Only" political primary election process was unconstitutional, and the Supreme Court, also, ruled in the James V. Martinship.

www.ingramcontent.com/pod-product-compliance
Lightning Source LLC
Chambersburg PA
CBHW020345130626
46549CB00003B/1293